Lead with Purpose:

A Memoir and Handbook for Leaders Ready to Serve, Heal, and Transform

Gloria A. Ramos

Publicatins printed in the United States

Dedication

To my husband Rey, my protector, my confidant, my best friend— this book is as much yours as it is mine. Before the world saw my light, you guarded it. Before I could believe in my own voice, you held it sacred. From bodyguard to beloved, you have stood by me without demand or expectation—only presence, only loyalty, only love. You have made the impossible feel attainable, the heavy feel manageable, and the ordinary feel sacred. You fill my coffee, warm my car, pack my trunk—and never once ask for recognition. You see what I carry, and you choose, every day, to carry it with me. You came when I needed safety. You stayed when I needed strength. And you never once asked me to shrink. Thank you for making space for my dreams, for reflecting my power back to me in a way that makes me feel cherished, not burdened. Because of you, I have achieved goals it took me fifty years to even attempt. Because of you, I know what it means to be fully supported. This book exists because you believed I could write it. You are home. And I am eternally grateful.

With all my love,
Gloria

"Ours is not the task of fixing the entire world all at once,
but of stretching out to mend the part of the world that is within our reach."

—Clarissa Pinkola Estés

Foreward

Leadership is more important than ever in today's times. It's a must if you're going to make a difference, help change things, and be an inspiration and of service to others. It is so essential that you realize that we are all born leaders in many different capacities. You can step into these gifts at any time and have a new way of living on purpose in the world.

In all of my years of studying and applying personal and business development, I have found that absorbing as much great information and knowledge as you can is extremely powerful for your success. This is followed by deep reflection through thinking, journaling, working with a coach, therapist or someone who can help you heal old traumas. This can be a lifelong journey, but starting, and making it a habit is a must. Finally, taking action is key, even when you think that you have no idea what you're doing. The practice of doing it creates positive power, thus making you a leader. As you continue to lead, you become better, and after thousands of hours you become an expert.

As you start your journey toward leadership and success, remember that being a leader is not a solo effort, but a collaborative one. We are all in this together. Leadership is about connection, community, and celebrating, supporting, and encouraging humanity.

This book memoir and workbook all in one by Gloria Ramos is an excellent, unique and very deep and thorough guide to becoming a leader that aligns with who you are. She does this through wisdom, personal stories, exercises and tools that you can immediately apply to your life.

May you shine bright as the true leader you are, with belief in yourself, your community and in positive change in the world.

Kim Somers Egelsee
Tedx Speaker, Publisher, 10x Best Selling Author
www.kimlifecoach.com

Table of Contents

Introduction

I never planned to lead. I planned to survive.

To make it through childhood with my voice intact. To raise my children with love—even when I wasn't sure how to love myself. To protect my peace in systems that weren't built for women like me—let alone women with my story.

And yet…here I am.
A policymaker.
A mother.
A mentor.
A business owner.

A woman who walked through fire—and didn't just survive but returned with the blueprint.

This book is for the person inside you who's been leading longer than you've admitted. The one who keeps showing up, not for applause, but because you can't turn away. The one who's tired of choosing between service and self. The one who senses that the world won't truly change until we learn how to lead from a deeper place—one rooted in wholeness, not performance.

You don't need more hustle.
You need healing.
You need truth.
You need alignment.
You need the kind of leadership that begins within

and expands outward—not as control, but as influence. Not as perfection, but as presence.

This is not a book about leadership strategies. It's a book about becoming It's about remembering your sacred role in the world. It's about choosing to stop performing and start embodying. It's about the truth that your story—yes, even the parts you've wanted to hide—is the foundation of your authority. You are the legacy You are the answer someone else is praying for. And everything you've endured can become a gift—if you learn how to lead from it.
Let's begin.

Part 1: The Heart of True Leadership

Why True Leaders Serve First — and Get Inspired in the Process

Chapter 1: Leadership Is About Service

"Service is the rent we pay for the privilege of living on this earth."
— Shirley Chisholm

Elevating Others, Creating Impact

I used to think leadership meant being in charge. Being the one with the answers. The one who could fix it, carry it, handle it — alone.

Turns out, that belief nearly broke me.

Because being "in charge" without being in service will leave you empty, exhausted, and eventually resentful. And it won't just harm you — it'll quietly drain the inspiration from everyone around you.

I learned this not in a boardroom, but in my home. There was a time when I was working two jobs, raising my children alone, serving on boards, organizing communities, and showing up strong for everyone... but secretly falling apart. I thought I was being a great leader. I thought leading meant always being "on," always being reliable, always putting out fires and fixing things.

What I didn't realize was this: I was leading from depletion, not overflow. And people don't get inspired by your perfection — they get inspired by your presence.

I had to unlearn performance and re-learn service. Not service as martyrdom. But service as a connection. Service as energy. Leadership that inspires instead of impresses.

And it started the moment I asked myself: "Who am I really helping — and am I helping them rise, or just keeping myself busy?"

That question changed everything.

What Leadership Is — and What It's Not

Let's clear something up: Not everyone in a position of power is a leader. And just because someone can manage a team, run a business, or win an election doesn't mean they know how to lead people well.

A title doesn't make you a leader. A platform doesn't make you a leader. Even having a following on social media doesn't make you a leader.

Leadership is about how you show up when it's inconvenient. It's about how you make people feel when they are around you. It's about what happens when no one is clapping, but you still serve anyway.

See, we've got too many folks out here trying to look important instead of being impactful. They chase control. They hoard credit. They lead through fear, manipulation, or charm — whatever gets them the result.

But that's not leadership. That's theater.

Real leadership? It's service in motion. It's showing up with integrity when it would be easier to stay quiet. It's giving people a sense of safety, clarity, and direction when the world feels chaotic.

When you lead from service, you inspire others — not because you're perfect, but because you're present. You're clear, consistent, and courageous.

The Three Types of Leadership That Inspire and Serve

In my life — from raising kids to serving on school boards to running businesses — I've seen a lot of leadership. Some of it inspiring, a lot of it disappointing. But the ones that really stick? The ones that move people, change lives, and leave a legacy? They all had one thing in common: they served first.

In the next few chapters, we'll dive into three kinds of leadership I've seen heal families, transform communities, and ignite movements. They're not fancy. They're not loud. But they are real.

Let me introduce them to you:

- **Catalytic Leadership** – the kind that lights a spark and empowers others to move forward with boldness and clarity.

- **Adaptive Leadership** – the kind that stays steady when everything around you is shifting, uncertain, or painful.

- **Legacy Leadership** – the kind that isn't just about now, but about building something that lasts long after you're gone.

Each one of these styles serves a different purpose, but they all come back to the same truth: real leadership inspires people by how you serve them — not how you control them.

And the best part? You don't have to be famous, rich, or in a corner office to be that kind of leader.

You just must be you, with intention.

The Hardest Meeting of My Life — And I Showed Up Anyway

In 2014, I almost died.

Not metaphorically. Not emotionally. Clinically, medically — I flatlined for over two minutes.

I had double pneumonia. Sepsis. My lungs were operating at 65%. My heart was racing nonstop. My organs were failing. I couldn't breathe, couldn't speak more than a few words without coughing until I trembled. I was in the hospital for more than four weeks.

I broke four ribs from coughing. I was 42 years old — a single mom to a four-year-old son with autism and a ten-year-old daughter who struggled with auditory processing disorder and suicidal thoughts. I hadn't seen my babies in weeks. My body was in chaos, and so was the world around me.

I was completely alone.

And then the phone started ringing.

Reporters. Radio hosts. Community members. The Daily Breeze News Paper

They called, not to check on me, but to ask about a massive scandal breaking in our school district.

While I was fighting for my life, the very people I had trusted on the school board had betrayed the community. Our superintendent was allegedly stealing public funds. The story went national. And because I was part of the board, my name was now attached to it — painted with the same brush as those who had looked the other way, or worse.

I couldn't even speak, but I was suddenly asked to explain myself. To defend myself from something I hadn't done. To carry the weight of other people's silence and secrets.

I was already half-dead. And now I was being blamed for something I didn't even have the strength to fight back against.

So, you know what I did?

I checked myself out of the hospital. Fever, four broken ribs, weak lungs, and all.

I could barely form a sentence. I could barely stand. But I knew — that the people who still believed in me, even if they were unsure, needed to see my face.

So, I walked into that board meeting through the front door, with my two little kids at my side.

No one escorted me. No one welcomed me. The other board members snuck in through the back.

I sat my children in the front row of the audience and took my place at the dais — next to people who had hidden behind silence and strategy. I sat there, praying my kids could hold on just a few more hours while I tried to show my community who I really was.

Seven hours. That's how long that meeting lasted. Seven hours of insults. Yelling. People throwing things. People I had served for years are now questioning if I was just another dishonest politician.

I couldn't speak. I couldn't defend myself. So I just sat there.

And at that moment — I didn't feel like a hero. I didn't feel strong. I felt broken, exhausted, and humiliated.

But looking back now?

I know exactly what that moment was.

That was leadership. That was service in its rawest, realest form.

Because I didn't show up for applause. I didn't show up to be right. I showed up because it mattered. Because the people mattered. Because the truth mattered.

Even if no one could see it at the time.

That night, I didn't fix everything. It didn't clear my name or end the accusations. But it planted something deep in me. A knowing. A clarity. A kind of sacred strength I carry with me to this day:

I don't lead to be liked. I lead because I serve. I lead because I love. And no one gets to take that from me.

That's what leadership looks like.
It's not glamorous. It's not easy.
It's showing up when no one else does.

The Hardest Meeting of My Life.

Activation: Step Into Servant Leadership

Today, do one small thing that reflects true leadership. Not because you "should," but because it lights something up in you.

It might be:

- Encouraging someone you usually overlook
- Apologizing when you don't have to
- Offering support without expecting credit
- Asking someone how they really are — and listening

Then say this out loud — yes, say it out loud:

"I am a leader because I serve. I am not here to perform. I am here to inspire."

You don't have to be perfect to lead powerfully. You just have to be present — and willing to show up again tomorrow.

Chapter 2: Beliefs and Self-Awareness — *The Inner Work*

"Until you make the unconscious conscious, it will direct your life, and you will call it fate."
— Carl Jung

What you believe is true.

For a long time, I lived trapped inside the identity my circumstances forced on me — the survivor, the fighter, the one who kept it together when no one else could. On the outside, I wore the mask people wanted to see — strong, capable, sometimes even "good." But inside, I didn't feel protected. I didn't feel seen. I didn't feel safe.

I thought if I worked hard enough, proved myself enough, kept pushing long enough, I could outrun the parts of me I didn't want anyone to see. But no matter how far I climbed, some invisible weight pulled me back.

It took years — and more painful lessons than I ever imagined — to realize the truth: My past didn't define me. My beliefs about myself did.

And until I changed my inner blueprint, no title, no degree, no achievement would ever set me free.

Leadership doesn't begin the moment the world claps for you It begins in the quiet place where you choose who you are — and who you refuse to be.

Your Belief System: The Hidden Architecture of Leadership

Belief is not simply a personal matter. It is structural — the invisible framework that governs every move a leader makes.

Research in cognitive science and psychology shows that our beliefs create internal maps that direct perception, decision-making, and behavior. They influence how we interpret stress, how we approach risk, how we trust, and how we navigate relationships — all critical elements in sustainable leadership.

Your belief system is the engine driving your leadership. It determines:

- How far you will allow yourself to go.
- How deeply you will allow yourself to connect.
- How fiercely you will allow yourself to rise when the world feels heavy.

Most leadership training focuses on external strategies — better communication, sharper decision-making, clearer vision. But underneath every tool and tactic is belief: the quiet, often unquestioned assumptions about worth, safety, power, and possibility.

If you believe you are worthy, resilient, and capable, you subconsciously move toward growth and opportunity. If you believe you are unsafe, unseen, or unworthy, you subconsciously shrink, sabotage, or settle.

This is not theory. It is biological. Studies in neuroplasticity confirm that belief systems are not fixed. They are malleable — reinforced or rewritten by repeated experiences and emotional conditioning. Each decision you make — every conversation you navigate, every risk you choose to take or avoid — sends a signal to your brain about who you are and what is possible.

Beliefs are not intellectual ideas. They are embodied experiences. They are etched into your neural networks, reinforced by the emotional states you practice most often.

When your belief system is rooted in fear or scarcity, no external success will feel sustainable. You will keep leading from survival, no matter how impressive the resume looks.

Self-awareness is not optional for leaders.

It is the first and most important act of leadership.

It demands honest inquiry:

- Whose voice am I leading with?
- Whose fears still inform my decisions?
- Whose limits have I mistaken for truth?

You do not have to dismantle yourself to lead at a higher level. You have to dismantle the belief systems that no longer serve the leader you are becoming.

When you commit to reshaping your inner architecture, you don't just lead more effectively — you lead from a place that creates lasting impact, resilience, and legacy.

Identity Is the Foundation That Cannot Be Faked

You can want success.
You can crave impact.
You can even achieve influence.

But unless your identity — your core sense of self — aligns with the life you are building, leadership will always feel brittle, defensive, and exhausting.

Research across behavioral psychology, including work from Dr. Albert Bandura and James Clear, confirms that lasting behavior change is identity-driven. It is not enough to set bigger goals. You must embody the kind of person for whom those goals feel natural and inevitable.

Identity is the foundation.

If you believe you are inadequate, no title will ever silence the doubt. If you believe you are here to create meaningfully, no setback will have the power to erase your vision.

You can master every leadership tactic available — but if the self you return to under pressure is still negotiating your worth, your leadership will always fracture when it matters most.

True leadership is not built by layering new strategies on top of old fractures. It is built by returning to the foundation and reinforcing it until it can carry the weight of who you are becoming.

Identity is not static. Neuroscience shows that identity is a network of habitual thoughts, emotions, and behaviors — subject to change through conscious repetition and emotional investment.

You are not trapped by who you were. You are shaped by what you continue to practice.

Until your identity matches the future you are creating, leadership will feel like a fight for survival. When your identity shifts, leadership becomes an expression of presence — not effort.

It doesn't mean the work gets easier. It means you become the kind of person who can carry it differently.

The leader people trust most is not the one with the most polished strategies. It's the one whose presence feels congruent — whose inner architecture matches their outer voice.

This is the real foundation. And it cannot be faked. So where do we go from here?

Small Actions, Big Legacy: *The Neuroscience of Casting Votes*

Leadership is not built in one defining moment. It is built in thousands of small, often unseen decisions.

Modern neuroscience — particularly in studies of experience-dependent neuroplasticity — shows that our brains physically rewire based on repeated experiences .Every action reinforces a pathway. Every choice casts a vote for the identity you are practicing into reality.

You don't need radical overnight change to become a different kind of leader. You need consistency.

Each time you choose integrity over comfort, you strengthen the neural pathways that expect and demand character. Each time you honor a commitment when no one is watching, you build internal evidence that trust is not situational — it is structural.

Leadership is formed in the quiet places:

- Choosing honesty when no one would blame you for hiding
- Extending mentorship when there is no immediate reward
- Resting before exhaustion forces you to — because sustainability is a leadership responsibility, not a luxury

These small actions accumulate.

Over time, the mind, the body, and even the emotional field around you begin to organize around the leader you have steadily become.

The work is not glamorous.
It is not performative.
It is cellular.

Every action is a signal. Every signal shapes expectations. And expectation, reinforced enough times, becomes identity.

When you treat every small moment as a vote for the future you are building, leadership becomes less about willpower and more about inevitability.

You are not faking it until you make it. You are embodying it until it's real.

This is how legacies are built — not through grand gestures, but through sustained alignment between belief, action, and presence.

Energy, Biology, and the Leadership You Broadcast

Leadership is not only about strategies and decisions. It is biological. It is energetic.

What you believe, feel, and think is not hidden. It becomes part of the atmosphere you create — felt before it is ever spoken.

Research in quantum biology shows that emotional states regulate the chemical environment of the body. Every thought, every feeling, every sustained emotional pattern releases neurotransmitters, hormones, and peptides that either fortify or diminish your internal coherence.

When fear and resentment dominate, cortisol floods the system — shrinking creativity, narrowing perception, and amplifying threat responses. When gratitude, clarity, and resilience are practiced, oxytocin and dopamine are released — expanding your ability to think flexibly, connect authentically, and act with vision.

Meanwhile, studies in heart-brain coherence demonstrate that the emotional rhythms of the heart shape cognitive function, decision-making, and even influence the electromagnetic field we unconsciously project into a room.

Leadership energy is not accidental. It is the biological and energetic consequence of what you rehearse internally.

When you lead from exhaustion, guardedness, or unresolved fear, you narrow the field around you. You limit what others feel possible in your presence.

When you lead from coherence, authenticity, and emotional regulation, you widen the field. You invite resilience, trust, and collaboration without needing to demand it.

You do not have to announce your leadership. You embody it. The emotional state you cultivate is not simply personal. It becomes structural. It influences every interaction, every opportunity, every future outcome.

The energy you broadcast — consciously or unconsciously — sets the parameters for the world you are leading.

Becoming Whole: My Fight for a Future

There was a time in my life when the world saw me through a lens of judgment I couldn't control. At forty years old, I was arrested and charged with a double violent felony — an accusation that painted me as someone I didn't even recognize.

I faced twenty-one years in prison. I had an eight-year-old daughter, a two-year-old son, and a future that felt like it was slipping through my fingers.

What most people didn't understand was that the so-called "violent" act was the instinct of a mother protecting her children. A woman — a distant family member tied to painful parts of my past — showed up at my home uninvited and crossed boundaries that triggered every alarm in my body. When she became physically aggressive, I reacted — not out of rage, but out of survival.

At that time, I was already an elected official. I stood behind the podium. I had spoken in rooms where people looked to me for leadership. But inside, I hadn't yet built the kind of leadership that sustains you when the bottom falls out.

In those months, I wasn't thinking about legacy. I was thinking about survival. I was thinking about protecting my children, reclaiming my life, and somehow staying whole.

I couldn't control the judgment. I couldn't undo the shame. But I could do the only thing that mattered: I could go inward. I faced the parts of myself the world tried to shame. I rebuilt my sense of self, one prayer, one breath, one honest choice at a time.

It was during that time — in the deepest surrender — that I remembered who had carried me all along. It wasn't my strength that rebuilt me. It was God that rebuilt me.

I surrendered the life I thought I had to protect. I surrendered the story others tried to place on me. And in that surrender, I found something stronger than survival: I found my true foundation.

I realized that leadership is not earned by appearances or titles. It is cast in the unseen choices — the ones you make when no one is watching and nothing feels certain.

That's why I wrote this handbook.

Not to teach you how to lead perfectly, under perfect circumstances. But to remind you: leadership is already inside you.

It's shaped in the moments you think might break you. It's refined when you stop asking for validation and start living from conviction.

This is not a manual for perfection. It's a guide for leaders who are willing to build something real — from the inside out. Because the world doesn't need leaders who have never fallen. It needs leaders who know how to rise.

And that rise always begins within.

I thought I had to be tough, do it all. It was how I valued myself.

Activation: Reclaiming the Leader Within

Leadership is not something you earn through achievement. It is something you reclaim through alignment.

Today, take one intentional action that strengthens the core identity you are choosing to live into — not the identity shaped by old wounds or survival, but the one shaped by your higher values, your deeper calling, and your true self.

Ask yourself:

- Where have I been leading from protection, rather than from conviction?
- What belief about myself needs to be retired — not because it was wrong for the past, but because it does not belong to my future?
- What small action today would reflect the leader I am becoming, not the one I once needed to be?
-

Then choose one brave, simple act:

- Speak one truth you used to hide.
- Set one boundary you once thought you didn't deserve.

- Stand one moment taller in the space you have already been called to occupy.

“The most powerful leadership tool you have is your own personal example.”
— John Wooden

Each choice is a new signal —to your mind, your body, your spirit — that you are no longer leading from fear. You are leading from truth.

Reflection:

Healing the Identity Beneath the Strategy.

- Where have old wounds shaped how I see myself and what I believe I deserve?

- In what ways have I armored myself in order to survive — and what is it time to lay down?

- What part of my leadership still runs on proving something to others — and what would change if I no longer needed to prove anything?

- What new belief about who I am is ready to be practiced, embodied, and lived?

You are not being asked to forget what you've survived. You are being invited to rise from it.

Leadership built on fear eventually fractures. Leadership built on truth, trust, and surrender to something greater than yourself creates legacy.

The work begins inside. And everything you build outward will rise from there.

Chapter 3: Catalytic Leadership

***"The most common way people give up their power is by thinking they don't have any."* — Alice Walker**

Be the Match That Lights the Fire

My niece was one of the latter.

By the time she came to live with me during her senior year of high school, she'd already been counted out. She had bounced between schools. She'd even tried one of those old-school military-style academies — the kind meant to "straighten girls out" more than lift them up. But no one had really taken the time to understand her, the pain or the drive within her. To see who she was beneath all that struggle.

Except me.

She was a late bloomer — the kind of student who took a little longer to finish things, who needed space to find her rhythm. But I always knew. I felt it in my spirit the moment she entered the world and still the day she entered my home. There was *fire* in her. Gentle, determined, sacred fire. She didn't need fixing. She needed someone to look her in the eyes and say, *"I see you. And I believe in who you're becoming."*

She graduated from one of the high schools in the district where I serve as a board trustee. And then she began the long, quiet, gritty eight-year journey to become a Los Angeles Police Officer.

She made it.

Not because of me — but because I saw what no one else was willing to look for. Because I held the mirror up long enough for her to see herself as capable. As worthy. As powerful.

She is not just a professional. She is not just a police officer. **She is a generational curse breaker**. A leader. A woman who rose — and stayed risen.

And that's the truth about catalytic leadership: You don't make people rise. You just show them it's possible. You hold the spark. And then, *you let them catch fire.*

A catalytic leader is someone who sparks growth, transformation, and confidence in others by believing in their potential, empowering their independence, and creating space for them to rise. They don't lead for recognition — they lead to activate purpose in the people around them.

My niece, the generational curse breaker!

What It Means to Be a Catalytic Leader

Catalytic leaders are sparks.

They lead with presence. With belief. With boldness rooted in love.

Catalytic leaders create movement — in people, in purpose, in possibility. They shake up the air in a room without yelling. They inspire people to think differently, speak boldly, and take action they might have been too afraid to take on their own, and they show people their own superpowers.

They hold the torch or others to take. They light the flame in others — and then *step back* so those people can carry it forward on their own.

That's the heartbeat of catalytic leadership: It's not about getting others to follow you. It's about helping them discover they can lead themselves.

These are the leaders who:

- Say, "I see more in you" — and mean it.
- Offer opportunity, then *release* control so others can rise.
- Speak life into people's potential — and don't need the credit for it.
- Are willing to go first, to risk first, to speak first — so someone else doesn't have to be afraid to try.

Catalytic leadership doesn't require a title. It doesn't require applause. It requires *vision*, *discernment*, and *trust* — in yourself, in the people you serve, and in the timing of transformation.

How Catalytic Leadership Heals Others

This kind of leadership can change everything — especially for people who've been invisible.

You don't always know who's watching you. You don't always know who's struggling to see themselves as capable. But one small moment — one opportunity, one word of belief, one invitation to rise — can shift the entire course of someone's life.

Catalytic leadership heals because it:

- Validates the people who've gone unseen.
- Gives permission to speak, dream, and stretch.
- Restores dignity to people who've only ever been tolerated, not celebrated.

Most people don't need a lecture. They need someone to say, *"You don't have to be perfect to be powerful."* Catalytic leaders don't just make space — they *protect* it, so others can safely grow into who they're meant to be.

How Catalytic Leadership Heals the Leader

Here's the part we don't talk about enough:

Helping others rise also heals the one who leads.

When you become the mirror that reflects someone's light — without trying to outshine them — you start to see your own value with more clarity.

When you stop trying to be the savior and start trusting people to own their greatness, you release the pressure of always having to carry it all.

Catalytic leaders don't need to be needed. They want others to *outgrow them*. To move beyond them. To flourish on their own terms. And when that happens? There's no bitterness. Just joy. Just fulfillment. Just *freedom*.

Because catalytic leaders aren't building kingdoms for themselves — they're building capacity in others. They know that real legacy is measured in multiplication, not control.

This kind of leadership transforms the question from:

"How can I get people to follow me?" to *"How can I empower people to lead, with or without me?"*

That shift brings peace. It removes the burden of performing. It brings back the *why*. Catalytic leaders find purpose in planting seeds they may never see fully bloom — and still, they plant anyway.

The Secret Sauce: It's Not About the Stage

Here's what I love most about catalytic leadership. You don't need a microphone. You don't need a title. You don't need permission.

You just need:

- Belief in someone else's potential
- Consistency in how you show up
- The courage to go first

Whether you're a teacher, a parent, a mentor, a coach, or someone just trying to do right by your circle — if you're willing to show up, speak truth, and hold space for someone to rise, you're already doing it.

You are already leading. And you're doing it in a way that leaves people stronger, not smaller. That's catalytic leadership. That's the kind of leadership that *heals the world*. One spark at a time.

Real Life in Action: Becoming the Leader I Already Was

My résumé wasn't remarkable.

But I showed up. I cared. I followed through. And still, every time a leadership opportunity came up, I stepped back.

Not because I didn't want it — but because somewhere along the way, I believed I wasn't supposed to want more. I believed I didn't deserve it.

I had been told I was "too rebellious." That I didn't have "the right kind of presence." That I needed to speak softer, act more agreeable, and lead more like… well, them.

But I'm different. It took me half a century, but today, I finally see what they couldn't. I see someone who is strong in spirit *and* in voice. A leader who doesn't need to posture or perform. Someone who cares more about doing the work than being seen doing it.

And what happened?

I stepped into myself. I stopped trying to be anyone else. I spoke clearly — and the room listened.

I shared my vision — and people leaned in. I brought calm, direction, and clarity. You could feel the shift.

Later that day, someone said to me,

"You're the first person who ever gave me a chance to lead without making me feel like I had to become someone else."

That moment lit her up — but it healed something in me, too.

Because that's what catalytic leadership does. You don't need to perform. You don't need to fix. You just need to see someone's fire, trust it, and give it room to breathe.

The right spark at the right moment can change a life. And when you help someone rise, a part of you rises too.

Activation: Becoming the Spark

Think of one person in your life right now who needs your belief. It might be someone overlooked, underestimated, or just deeply tired.

Do one thing this week to *spark* something in them:

- Invite them to lead something — even something small.
- Speak life into a gift they don't fully own yet.
- Say, "I see you. You don't have to become someone else to be powerful."

And then turn that same grace toward yourself.

"It is not the strongest of the species that survives, nor the most intelligent, but the one most responsive to change."
— Charles Darwin

Say this out loud, with your full voice:

"I am not here to perform. I am here to spark.
I lead to multiply, not to control. My presence is enough. My voice matters. And I make room for others to rise."

You're already the catalyst. All that's left is to own it — and keep showing up like it.

Reflection

Take a breath.
Now ask yourself:

- Where in your life have you dimmed your voice to make others more comfortable?
- Who saw something in you before you saw it in yourself?
- Who in your circle is quietly waiting to be invited into their power?
- Are you willing to be the person who lights their fire?

Let the answers rise. No judgment. Just truth.

Chapter 4: Adaptive Leadership – Grounded Enough to Change

"It is not the strongest of the species that survives, nor the most intelligent—it is the one most adaptable to change." — Charles Darwin

Boss: The Original Blueprint

We called her "Boss" — she earned that. She was my grandmother, and she led our family and our business with grit, grace, and unfailing devotion. Her name was Connie, but everyone knew her by how she moved through the world — steady, direct, compassionate, and always one step ahead of whatever life threw her way.

She inherited a struggling maple syrup and step stool company from her father, and transformed it into a thriving bar supply business that served restaurants, bars, and liquor stores across the region. This was in a time when women were not encouraged to be entrepreneurs. She left her husband in the 1950s — with two teenage children in tow — and built something no one saw coming. She didn't sell alcohol, but she sold everything else you'd need to run a place that served it. And she did it with no excuses, no shortcuts, and no need for applause.

We all worked for her. My siblings, my mom, and my fourth cousin, who was cognitively slower. She cared for and employed this cousin with full dignity for over 25 years. She made sure everyone had a role. She made sure everyone felt useful. She led a family and a business the way great leaders do — by creating structure, expecting excellence, and offering grace when it was needed most.

She wasn't loud. She wasn't flashy, although she always had perfectly styled short red hair. But she was always paying attention and always looking out for us.

Her hands taught me how to work. Her deep blue eyes taught me how to see. Her heart taught me what leadership really looks like.

She passed away at 96. Not a day goes by that I don't miss her — or try to live up to the standard she quietly set.

She didn't read leadership books. She didn't give TED Talks. She lived that term, adaptive leadership, long before it was a thing.

She inherited a failing family business — and adapted it into a thriving enterprise. When syrup and step stools weren't enough to survive, she reimagined what was possible and pivoted into bar supplies. She didn't have consultants or spreadsheets. She had grit, a sharp eye for what worked, and the confidence to try something new when the old way didn't serve.

When her marriage ended, she didn't collapse. She adjusted. She raised two kids on her own, ran deliveries, kept books, and led a team — all without ever complaining that it was too much. She never waited for the world to become more fair or convenient. She simply met life on its terms and kept moving.

She adapted to the business. She adapted to the family. And she adapted herself to every season of responsibility, never losing her sense of dignity or grace.

She just showed up — in every storm — and led with unwavering truth.

She was my first model of adaptive leadership.

And she remains my greatest one.

The Original Blueprint: Boss

The Science and Soul of Adaptive Leadership

Adaptive leadership is rooted in the ability to stay present in complexity and lead with clarity, even when certainty is not available. It's a skillset — and a mindset — that comes from understanding how people and systems truly work.

Instead of leading through rigid rules or top-down demands, adaptive leadership recognizes that people, teams, and institutions are dynamic and responsive — more like ecosystems than machines. They respond to pressure, emotion, trust, and change. Leaders who understand this create space for transformation by making room for learning, discomfort, and new thinking — even when the path ahead is unclear.

The power of adaptive leadership is confirmed both by modern science and the hard-earned wisdom of real-world experience.

Complexity theory shows that in uncertain environments, solutions emerge through connection, not control. Organizational psychology tells us that growth happens in cultures where people feel safe enough to challenge assumptions and take risks. Neuroplasticity research confirms that repeated choices rewire the brain — including the way we lead, respond, and relate. And leadership studies highlight that sustainable influence comes from emotional intelligence, not just strategy.

Adaptive leadership equips people to do the hard work of evolving — to think critically, respond intentionally, and stay engaged through discomfort. It teaches leaders to notice patterns, regulate tension, and invite shared ownership instead of carrying everything alone. It values deep listening, reflective thinking, and courageous decision-making.

There are core tools adaptive leaders rely on, first introduced by Ronald Heifetz, Marty Linsky, and Alexander Grashow:

- **Zoom Out to See Clearly**: Step away from the immediate noise so you can observe the bigger picture — patterns, relationships, and what's not being said. Notice what's playing out beneath the surface. Adaptive leaders resist the urge to react and instead look for patterns.
- **Name the Real Problem**: Understand whether the issue requires a quick solution or a deeper shift in mindset, behavior, or culture. Not all problems need the same response. Some require expertise. Others require emotional labor, mindset shifts, and learning.
- **Regulate Distress**: Keep the pressure high enough to encourage growth, but not so high it causes burnout or rebellion.
- **Stay with What Matters**: Don't let discomfort push people back into avoidance. Keep focus on the real issue long enough for transformation to happen. Stay with the hard conversation. Don't let the room drift back into avoidance.

- **Invite Others to Rise**: Stop solving everything yourself. Let others take ownership and grow into their own leadership. Empower others to rise. Stop fixing and start facilitating.
- **Honor the Voices at the Edge**: Change often starts with the people others ignore. Make space for truth-tellers and protect the courage it takes to speak up. Listen to the truth-tellers. Change rarely comes from the top — it emerges from the edge.

These tools may sound simple, but applying them with integrity is not easy. They require emotional intelligence, humility, and a willingness to evolve right alongside those you lead.

What makes adaptive leadership especially powerful today is how deeply it speaks to both the social and personal climate we're in.

We live in a time where misinformation spreads faster than truth, where algorithms reward outrage, and where authority is often confused with charisma. In this world, adaptive leaders become a kind of anchor. They discern rather than react. They ask better questions. They hold space for nuance. They don't pretend to know everything, but they know how to hold people steady while new clarity is being born.

And while adaptive leadership is often discussed in organizational settings, it also has profound implications for personal healing.

Many of us were raised in environments that didn't reward reflection. We were taught to be quick, perform strength, and protect our image. Adaptive leadership interrupts that conditioning. It asks us to lead from wholeness, not from habit. It invites us to explore the beliefs we carry — about worth, power, conflict, trust — and to redefine them through lived practice.

When leaders begin to embody adaptive leadership at a soul level, healing happens — not only in those they serve, but within themselves. Because they're no longer performing leadership. They're becoming it.

This kind of leadership has no interest in hierarchy for hierarchy's sake. It values dignity. It rewards growth. It does not need to be the loudest voice in the room — just the most grounded.

If you're still here, reading this page, you already know something in you is being prepared.

Not for polished perfection, but for presence. Not to dominate the room, but to hold the room. Not to offer answers, but to ask the questions that lead us somewhere new.

You don't need a new map. You need the courage to move forward while drawing one.

This is adaptive leadership. And it will meet you exactly where you are.

Leading Without a Map: A Mother's Adaptation

When my son was two and a half years old, he was nearly nonverbal. There was no clear diagnosis, no roadmap to follow — just long, quiet stretches where I knew he had thoughts, ideas, and needs but no way to express them.

In my experience, nothing will stretch your capacity for leadership more than trying to help your child communicate when the world doesn't yet speak their language.

So, I began building a way for us to understand each other.

I used Scrabble letters, magnets, and a large blackboard to create a visual space where he could begin to physically shape his thoughts. It wasn't a textbook strategy — just something I felt might work. Over time, letters became words, and words became full expressions. What started as an improvised solution turned into a bridge — not just for language, but for connection.

What I know now after that experience is that leadership often shows up in the quietest places. Not in the systems that are handed to us, but in the ones we create when we refuse to give up on understanding someone fully.

Today, my son is thriving in high school. He's perceptive, articulate, and richly expressive. His insight isn't just sharp — it's layered. He listens differently. He observes deeply. And he continues to teach me how to lead without needing control.

Adaptive leadership taught me — and continues to remind me — that we don't need to know everything to be effective. We just need to stay attuned, stay present, and keep adapting to what's true in front of us.

Activation: Practice Adaptive Leadership in Your Life

This week, notice one situation in your life that feels uncertain or out of your control — whether it's in your work, your family, or your own internal state.

Instead of trying to fix it right away, pause. Zoom out. Ask yourself:

- What patterns am I seeing?
- What's really being asked of me here?
- What part of me wants to react — and what part is ready to respond?

Then, choose one small adaptive move:

- Ask a better question.
- Invite someone else's insight instead of solving alone.
- Hold space for discomfort without rushing to resolution.

This is how adaptive leadership grows — in quiet choices, repeated over time.

Reflection:

Deepening the Inner Work

- Where in my life am I still trying to lead with control instead of curiosity?
- When have I avoided discomfort instead of staying present with it?
- Who in my life has modeled adaptive leadership for me — and what did I learn from them?
- What part of me still believes I need to have all the answers to lead well?

Let this reflection be honest. Let it stretch you. Adaptive leadership doesn't ask you to be perfect. It invites you to be fully here — with integrity, humility, and room to grow.

That's enough.

That's powerful.

That's leadership.

Chapter 5: Legacy Leadership — Building for Generations

***"Society grows great when old men plant trees in whose shade they know they shall never sit."* — Greek Proverb**

"Lead Beyond Your Lifetime"

Legacy leadership is not a future concept—it is a present responsibility. It's embedded in the decisions we make when no one is watching, in how we navigate tension with grace, and in the way we uphold our values under pressure. Every act of integrity is a seed. Every principled stand taken—especially in spaces where compromise is easier—is a brick in the foundation of something that can endure.

In a culture built on immediacy and optics, where reward is often determined by visibility and profit, legacy asks us to think in longer timelines. It requires us to extend our vision beyond quarterly goals, beyond professional milestones, and into the lived experiences of the generations that will inherit what we've built—or neglected.

To lead with legacy in mind is to acknowledge that our work, our choices, and our character shape more than our reputation. They shape the world. This chapter is about anchoring your leadership in long-term vision—one that outlives your position, your platform, and even your lifetime.

The Architecture of Enduring Leadership

Legacy leadership is expansive. It recognizes that impact is not limited to moments of recognition, but measured by the depth of the values instilled in others. A true legacy is not crafted in a rush; it is cultivated through intention, clarity, and a willingness to consider others in the arc of our decisions.

The measure of your leadership is not just in how many people follow you today, but in how many will be strengthened by the ripple effects of your example tomorrow. This means mentoring without attachment, serving without the need for validation, and investing in people and systems you may never personally benefit from.

Ask yourself:

- What principles am I reinforcing through my daily conduct?
- How do I respond when leadership requires patience over performance?
- What conditions am I creating for others to thrive, especially those who may never know my name?

Legacy leadership is an act of generosity. It invites you to design systems, cultivate cultures, and nurture people in ways that uplift their humanity, not just their productivity. It refuses to extract value from people for the sake of personal gain, and instead builds environments where value multiplies across time.

Consider the leaders who shaped your life—not necessarily the ones with accolades, but the ones whose steadiness, compassion, or wisdom still echo in your decisions. Those individuals shaped more than moments; they shaped your trajectory. That is the heartbeat of legacy leadership.

It's not theoretical. It's deeply human. It's knowing that our leadership either builds bridges or burns them. And it is our responsibility to choose wisely—not just for ourselves, but for the people we love, the communities we serve, and the generations to come. Jane Goodall said it perfectly and to the point, ***"What you do makes a difference, and you have to decide what kind of difference you want to make."***

A Living Legacy: My Grandmother's Garden

I remember standing in my grandmother's backyard, nine years after she passed. I was preparing for my own wedding in the very garden she once tended—a home that held five generations of our family. The flowers were still blooming. Some of the very perennials she planted sixty years earlier lined the path I would walk to say my vows.

Her hands had shaped the soil that now held my new beginning.

She wasn't a public figure. She didn't author books or speak from stages. But her life taught us what consistency looked like. What humility felt like. What dignity in the face of hardship could offer. She led our family with care, expectation, and unwavering love.

Her legacy didn't need a plaque. It lived in the way we showed up for one another. In the standards we hold. In the traditions that still ground us.

Legacy isn't an abstract idea. It is a lived experience, passed through daily decisions and reinforced and protected by presence. It endures not because of noise, but because it was rooted in substance.

Before we close this chapter, take a moment to remember: legacy is not just about creation, it's about guardianship. What you build matters—but what you protect, what you preserve, and what you pass down through your presence matters just as much.

Grandma's Garden

Activation: Lead Beyond the Moment

Identify one area of your life where your leadership could extend beyond immediate outcomes. Ask yourself:

- Who is affected by how I show up here?
- What values would I want someone to absorb just by observing me?

Take one action this week that reflects your commitment to legacy—whether it's mentoring someone, clarifying your values in writing, or realigning a project with your long-term vision.

Then speak this truth aloud: "I am a legacy leader. I lead with generations in mind. My leadership is rooted in values, guided by vision, and protected through action. What I build, I also preserve."

Reflection:

Building What Outlasts You

- If someone mirrored my leadership entirely, what would their life look like?
- What stories do I want told about how I made people feel?
- What will my leadership make possible for someone I may never meet?
- What do I need to let go of building something that lasts?

Legacy doesn't require perfection. It requires presence, intention, and the courage to lead as if your life matters beyond your timeline.

- What part of my legacy needs protection—not just planning?
- How can I safeguard the values, stories, and sacrifices that brought me here?

Part 2: What Leadership is NOT

"Leadership is not about being in charge. It is about taking care of those in your charge."
—Simon Sinek

Chapter 6: When Leadership Wounds Instead of Heals

***"Be careful not to become the very thing you are fighting against."* —Angela Davis**

"Recognizing the Cost of Leading from Ego"

It didn't happen in a dramatic explosion. It happened in a thousand small silences. In the meetings where my input was asked but never truly considered. In the public affirmations that never translated to private support. In the hollow compliments that disguised discomfort with my presence, my power, my pace.

It's strange how clearly you can feel something shift without having the language for it. I didn't call it ego at the time. I called it pressure. I called it culture. I called it leadership.

But what I was witnessing wasn't leadership—it was performance. And what I was experiencing wasn't collaboration—it was subtle control. And what I carried afterward wasn't inspiration—it was fatigue laced with self-doubt.

This chapter isn't about calling people out. It's about calling ourselves into something higher. Ego leads even the most well-intentioned leadership into terrain where people walk away diminished, not developed.

When Ego Replaces Presence

Ego isn't always loud. Sometimes it's the polished résumé that refuses to listen. Sometimes it's the flawless branding that hides a culture of fear. Sometimes it's the quiet dismissal of someone else's idea—because it wasn't yours.

The mistake many leaders make is confusing ego with strength. But ego isn't strength. It's armor. Strength listens. Ego dominates. Strength invites. Ego performs. Strength creates safety. Ego demands silence.

Psychologist and leadership researcher Dr. Jennifer Freyd coined the term "institutional betrayal"—the experience of being harmed not by the enemy, but by the very systems and people we expected to protect us. Ego-based leadership is often an invisible betrayal. It erodes trust not with one incident, but with a culture that teaches people their dignity is conditional.

And when people stay too long in that system, they begin to gaslight themselves. They wonder if they're overreacting. If their gut instinct is too sensitive. If they should just "get over it."

People aren't overreacting. They're overcompensating. For the lack of safety. For the absence of acknowledgment. For the fear that if they bring their whole self, it will cost them their seat.

The Neuroscience of Ego Leadership

The brain is a social organ. As Dr. Dan Siegel's research shows, our nervous systems are wired to seek safety in relationships. In environments where we feel seen, trusted, and valued, our prefrontal cortex—the center of decision-making and emotional regulation—lights up. Creativity flows. Learning expands. Risk-taking becomes possible.

In environments governed by ego, where approval becomes a transaction and feedback is weaponized, the amygdala—our fear center—takes over. Cortisol rises. Perspective narrows. People shift into survival mode.

This isn't philosophy. This is biology. You can't have vision when your team is in survival. You can't have innovation when people are performing safety instead of feeling it. You can't have real leadership if your presence is activating fight-or-flight responses in those around you.

When ego leads, the room shrinks—even when the room applauds.

I once worked with a brilliant community organizer—passionate, sharp, and deeply committed to justice. As his influence grew, so did his need to control everything. He stopped listening. He cut people off. He turned collaboration into a hierarchy of "who's most committed."

Eventually, his closest allies distanced themselves. He burned bridges—and blamed others for walking away. When I confronted him, he was defensive. But eventually he admitted something honest: "I was terrified they'd stop respecting me if I stopped performing."

He didn't need more titles. He needed more healing. He needed to remember that leadership rooted in ego cannot sustain liberation. He's still leading today—differently. He asks more questions. He centers others. He says, "I was wrong." And because of that? People are coming back.

The Cost of Controlled Composure

Not all ego in leadership is loud. Sometimes it wears a calm face. I've led entire rooms while managing internal exhaustion. Kept composure while carrying private grief. Delivered excellence while quietly feeling unseen.

But here's what I've learned: high-functioning depletion is still depletion. You can still lose connection without ever raising your voice. You can still cause harm while appearing poised. Because people feel our energy—even when we're saying all the right things.

I once completed a training that was technically flawless. The timing was sharp. The slides were polished. The delivery was efficient.

But afterward, a colleague pulled me aside and said gently, "You weren't really with us. You were just getting us through it."

That stayed with me. Because it's possible to perform leadership so well, we forget to embody it. It's possible to keep showing up for the work, and quietly disappear from the purpose.

This is the subtler side of ego leadership: Not arrogance. Not control. But performance without presence. Precision without real connection.

When Presence Becomes the Power

Brendon Burchard teaches that power is presence. And presence isn't about having the loudest voice in the room, it's about being rooted, clear, and intentional with your energy.

That moment after the training wasn't a failure. It was a signal. My systems were running—but I wasn't present in them. My clarity had dulled. My energy was low. I had raised the necessity for performance—but not for restoration.

In Brendon's six habits of high performance, the second is to generate energy. And that doesn't come from coffee or charisma. It comes from clarity, purpose, and full engagement.

When we're exhausted, we often think we need to do more. But what we really need is to feel again. To reconnect with the "why" underneath the work. To check in with the identity we're bringing into the room.

Presence is a habit. And like all habits, it must be trained, especially when the body is tired, and the calendar is full.

What helped me was going back to the foundations: • Clarity on how I wanted to show up • Energy to stay present, not just appear productive • Courage to acknowledge when I needed rest—not just results.

Because when we reclaim presence, we don't just become better leaders. We become aligned ones.

Understanding Shadow Work

Shadow work is the courageous practice of looking at the parts of ourselves we've exiled, rejected, or refused to acknowledge—the parts that operate beneath the surface but shape everything from our decisions to our leadership presence.

Our shadow doesn't mean we are bad. It means we are human.

These are the instincts and behaviors we suppress: envy, rage, control, superiority, shame, manipulation. They often stem from old wounds, unmet needs, or core beliefs formed in childhood.

When ignored, the shadow drives our leadership unconsciously. It shows up in self-righteousness, defensiveness, micromanagement, comparison, people-pleasing, and passive-aggressive behavior. But when brought into the light—through honest reflection, compassion, and accountability—the shadow loses its grip. We stop leading from our wounds and start leading from our wholeness.

This is not a one-time act—it's a lifelong discipline. Leaders who do shadow work consistently experience greater inner peace, clearer decision-making, and have a more powerful impact. Good leaders don't just perform alignment—they live it.

Understanding shadow work and presence go hand in hand. As Brendon teaches, energy and presence are high-performance habits. But without shadow work, those habits can become masks. To lead with clarity and energy, you must first reclaim the parts of yourself you've tried to outrun. That's where the real power is.

The Shadow I No Longer Need

There was a moment during my time as an elected official when everything in me screamed, *This is wrong.* A fellow board member—slick, persuasive, and deeply connected—was pushing a big energy contract that did not serve our district. It served his friend. It served his ego. But it did not serve our kids or our budget.

I opposed it. Fiercely. Visibly. Unapologetically.

And from that moment on, I became the enemy.

He positioned me as combative. Told others I was on a "power trip." Said I was making it personal. And to my horror, it worked. One by one, my colleagues turned. I was accused of grandstanding, shut out of decisions, and made into the villain in a story I didn't write.

I could sit here and give you all the facts: I *was* right. The contract would have cost us millions. I stood for fiscal responsibility, for ethics, for students. And I'd do it again. But here's the shadow truth I've come to own:

I wasn't just reacting to the deal.
I was reacting to betrayal.

To being misunderstood.
To being outnumbered.
To being bullied.

And when I felt threatened—when I felt that righteous flame—I didn't back down. I doubled down. My trauma-trained nervous system kicked in. Warrior mode. Precision. Armor. No mercy. I became so focused on ***being right*** that I lost access to the very grace I now lead from.

Yes, he was manipulative. Yes, the board was complicit. But I was not blameless. Why? Because even in our most righteous moments, our shadow rides shotgun.

Here's the truth I couldn't see then: I couldn't stand the bully in him because there was still a bully in me. Maybe not in that boardroom. Maybe not in that vote. But the part of me that got rigid, intense, unyielding when I felt threatened—that was my shadow. I wasn't just fighting others. I was fighting the unhealed parts of me.

If I had softened—just a little—maybe I wouldn't have lost so much ground. Not on the vote. But on the relationships. On my peace. On my health.

Because after the dust settled, I wasn't just tired. I was isolated. Ostracized. *Persona non grata.* And the warrior in me said, *Good. Let them be uncomfortable. I can outlast all of them.*

But the wiser part of me now knows: I won the battle. But I didn't win the room. And I definitely didn't win with God.

The moment we let our shadow go unexamined, our leadership becomes distorted—even when our values are sound.

What I've come to embody is this: we are responsible for all of it. Not just the things we say out loud. But the energy we bring. The blame we hold. The stories we cling to. We don't just attract chaos—we mirror it.

If you hate something in someone else, there's a good chance it's still hidden in you. And once you bring it to light, it loses its grip. That's how you reclaim your peace.

That doesn't mean we excuse wrongdoing. It means we investigate our part in the equation. Because only through shadow work can we move from opposition to alignment. From self-protection to God-connection.

I now meet those moments with grace. I protect my peace before my point. I forgive the woman who once led from her armor. And I honor the version of me who survived just long enough to become the woman writing these words.

The lesson? We are not just victims of leadership gone wrong. We are participants. And the only path to restoration is responsibility.

And that's not just my story. It's the headline every day.

Look around—at Congress, at school boards, at city councils. The game is blame. One side lobs accusations, the other strikes back harder. It's easier to perform outrage than to take responsibility. Easier to condemn than to self-reflect. Easier to fight than to feel.

But leadership is never won in the noise. It's shaped in the shadows. And sustained through the quiet, often lonely, act of personal accountability.

That moment on the board wasn't just about me and a contract. It was a mirror. A microcosm of what we're all swimming in: ego battles dressed up as public service, insecurity masquerading as policy, and a culture addicted to being right instead of being responsible.

So I say this to you, now that I've walked through it: The world may never apologize for its betrayals. Your opponents may never own their part. But if you want peace, if you want purpose, if you want true power—You must own *yours*. All of it.

Even the parts that didn't feel fair.
Even the parts shaped by trauma.
Even the parts that made you grit your teeth to admit.

We are responsible for our lives. All of it.
And neither you nor I need to lead from the shadows anymore.
We've outgrown the battle.
We're here for alignment.

The Shadow I No Longer Need.

Activation: Shadow Work in Leadership

This is a practice in seeing clearly—not to shame yourself, but to become more whole.

1. Name a recent moment when you felt irritated, threatened, or deeply righteous.
    - What part of the other person bothered you most?
    - What might that part be reflecting back to you?
1. Ask yourself: "Is there a version of this trait, tendency, or behavior in me?"
    - You're not excusing them. You're exploring your mirror.
1. Reclaim your leadership energy:
    - "What would it look like to lead with full presence, now that I've seen this shadow?"
    - "What would I choose if I felt safe enough to soften?"

Reflection:

• When has my leadership been fueled by fear or control, even if I didn't realize it at the time?

• What parts of me am I ready to reclaim, integrate, or release?

• What does leadership look like when it flows from presence, not performance?

Healing Affirmation: "I lead from wholeness, not from my wounds. My shadow is seen, my light is steady, and my leadership is rooted in truth."

Chapter 7: Boundaries, Clarity, and Power - Recognizing and Rising Above Toxic Leadership

"Not everyone deserves access to you. Peace is not a luxury. It's your currency."
—Gloria A. Ramos

Choosing Healing Over Hurt

I used to think toxic leadership was something you could outwork. That if I stayed excellent, stayed kind, stayed focused — I could outshine the dysfunction. I could rise high enough, perform hard enough, and maybe, just maybe, earn peace in the process.

But here's what no one tells you: You can't outwork toxicity that's rooted in fear. You can't heal a culture that rewards performance over presence, control over clarity, and silence over truth. And you can't protect your purpose if you keep sacrificing your peace to manage someone else's insecurity.

I've been in rooms where charm was currency and manipulation masked itself as vision. I've worked with leaders who punished honesty and celebrated compliance. And I've had to learn — not once, but over and over — how to rise without letting the poison in for too long. It will come in, but once we recognize it, we must flush it.

This chapter is about that exact edge. It's not about running away. It's about rising wisely. It's about knowing who you are, even when the room tries to convince you otherwise. It's about holding your center in systems that are spinning. Because sometimes the most sacred kind of leadership is staying whole in a place that's lost its way. Remember, "You don't have to set yourself on fire to keep others warm."

— Unknown

Being my momma's daughter grounds me when the world/workplace seems too toxic to handle.

When Leadership Hurts: How We Lose Ourselves — and How We Get Back

What Toxic Leadership Really Looks Like

Not every tough leader is toxic. Let's get that straight. Toxic leadership isn't about high standards or hard conversations. It's about control masquerading as care. It's about psychological manipulation wrapped in polished branding. It's about environments where people stop telling the truth because the truth costs too much.

It looks like:

- Leaders who hoard credit and distribute blame.
- Teams that confuse fear with respect.
- Organizations where speaking up means being shut out.
- Cultures that reward burnout and shame boundaries.

John Hoover names it for what it is: a system that erodes your clarity, steals your energy, and trains you to adapt to dysfunction as if it's normal.

Toxic leadership isn't always loud. Sometimes, it's subtle — a thousand tiny betrayals of integrity that chip away at your identity. And if you stay long enough, you begin to shape-shift — not into your highest self, but into a version of you that knows how to survive, not thrive.

How High Performers Lose Themselves in Toxic Systems

The most dangerous thing about toxic leadership isn't just what it does to the workplace. It's what it does to your internal compass.

High performers are especially vulnerable. Why? Because we don't like to fail. So, we adapt. We rationalize. We push harder. We overdeliver in an effort to restore the balance — not realizing the system is designed to keep us doubting.

You start working longer hours to prove you're valuable. You downplay your wins to avoid triggering resentment. You mute your instincts, second-guess your wisdom, and wake up wondering how you became someone who can't speak without permission.

And it goes deeper. Many of us came from environments where love had to be earned, where calm was conditional. So toxic workplaces feel familiar — even normal. We don't just tolerate them. We recreate our childhood patterns, believing that if we perform well enough, we'll finally be safe.

But here's the wake-up call: You do not need to dim your light to stay safe. You do not need to shrink your truth to survive dysfunction. You are not the problem just because you can see it clearly.

Staying Whole in a Fractured Culture

Here's how you hold the line when you're surrounded by leadership that leads from fear, ego, or insecurity:

1. Anchor in Identity
High performers root themselves in who they are before the system tries to rewrite their worth. Start every day with clarity:

- Who am I here to be?
- What values drive me?
- What won't I sacrifice? Because when the room gets chaotic, the grounded one becomes the leader — whether they have the title or not.

2. Protect Your Energy — Not Just Your Time
Hoover teaches: don't catch the disease. Meaning — don't mirror the dysfunction. Don't get pulled into gossip, cynicism, or reactive leadership just because it's all around you. You protect your energy by managing your nervous system — staying calm in meetings, breathing before you speak, walking away from bait. You protect your emotional clarity like it's your most sacred asset — because it is.

3. Don't Get Hooked by Approval or Reaction Toxic leaders often thrive on emotional bait. They know how to make you question yourself. They know how to create chaos so they can control the calm.

Your power? Don't bite. Don't argue to be understood. Don't perform to be praised. Don't shrink to be safe. Move with necessity — not ego. Keep your focus on service. On legacy. On the quiet work of staying aligned even when the room is misaligned.

4. Build Parallel Power

If you can't leave the system yet, build beside it. Start mentoring others. Create safe spaces within the chaos. Find your tribe — the ones who think like you, see like you, breathe like you. Erwin McManus would say: Don't become the very thing you're trying to heal. Stay true. Stay clean. Stay dangerous in your clarity.

But clarity doesn't always come easily. Especially when you're the only one speaking truth in a room that punishes it.

Communication Misfire and Course Correction

I've always told the truth. And I've paid for it.

There was a time I served on a board where I began to notice patterns—mismanagement, contradictions, behaviors that didn't add up. I brought my concerns forward, but instead of being heard, I was dismissed. They said I was too emotional. That things like this didn't happen "at our level." That I was seeing shadows where there were none.

The deeper betrayal wasn't just in what they ignored, it was in how they framed me for noticing.

And I broke. I lashed out—not with violence, but with words sharpened by exhaustion and disbelief. I spoke with disdain, frustration, and the kind of blunt force that doesn't invite understanding—it builds walls.

Here's the hard truth: I wasn't wrong. I had caught something real. Something serious. And time proved that. But who cares if you're right if no one is willing to listen?

That experience taught me something I wish I'd learned earlier: You don't persuade people by overpowering them. You don't build trust by trying to shame others into seeing what you see.

Brendon Burchard teaches that persuasion isn't about domination—it's about rapport. It's about aligning your message with someone's values, emotions, and readiness to understand. When you speak from depletion, even the truth sounds like an attack. But when you speak from clarity, it can actually move hearts, not just minds.

I still speak the truth. But now I do it from a different posture—one that leaves room for connection, not just correction. Because leadership isn't just about being right. It's about being heard.

Strong Enough to Walk Away

That wasn't the only time I spoke up. But it was one of the most painful. Eventually, I realized — clarity wasn't just about speaking. It was about choosing when to walk away.

There was a season in my leadership where I kept waiting for people to see me. To validate the work. To reward the service. To apologize for the manipulation. I thought if I was patient enough, loyal enough, consistent enough, something would change. - It didn't.

One day, I realized I was trading my integrity for their comfort. I was giving my light to people who only saw their own reflection.

So, I left. Not loudly. Not with vengeance. But with clarity. I stepped out, not because I was weak — but because I was finally strong enough to stop justifying smallness.

And from that space? Everything bloomed. My voice came back. My clarity sharpened. My leadership expanded — not in title, but in truth.

You don't always have to fight to win. Sometimes, you just must leave to live.

For the Budding Leader in a Toxic System

If you're growing in the shadows of toxic leadership, don't mistake dysfunction for destiny. You are not flawed because you recognize what's misaligned. The goal isn't to match the chaos—it's to rise above it with discernment and purpose. Let this chapter guide you in becoming the kind of leader you once longed for. Watch everything but internalize only what sharpens your integrity. Lead from the wisdom your wounds taught you—not the harm that caused them. That's how we end cycles. It will change your course!

Building a Leadership Practice That Heals, Not Harms

Healing from toxic leadership doesn't just mean leaving the dysfunction — it means building a new foundation of resilience, presence, and service-centered power. Experts in organizational psychology and leadership development agree: the best leaders aren't the ones who never break, but the ones who know how to integrate their pain into wisdom.

Harvard's Ronald Heifetz teaches that adaptive leadership — the capacity to thrive under pressure without losing integrity — is forged through self-regulation and reflection, not performance. Brene Brown reminds us that vulnerability is not weakness; it's the birthplace of courage. And emotional intelligence expert Daniel Goleman emphasizes that leaders who can recognize and manage their own emotions are the ones who create psychologically safe, high-performing cultures.

So, what does that mean for you? It means taking radical ownership of your nervous system. Practicing mindfulness not just to de-stress, but to build awareness. Learning to lead from core values — not from the need to be validated.

It means tracking where ego tries to hijack your clarity and returning — again and again — to your internal compass.

It means designing rhythms of recovery, not just rhythms of productivity. Because a healed leader leads differently. They create spaces where others feel safe to grow. They respond, rather than react. They hold the vision even when others are stuck in fear.

You don't need to be perfect. You just need to be present — to yourself, to your values, and to the people you're called to lead.

That is the legacy of a whole leader. And it starts here, with the choice to rise above without losing yourself.

Activation: Walking in Alignment

This week, take back one piece of yourself you've been handing over to toxic systems. It might be:

- Saying no to a meeting that drains you
- Telling the truth in a room that expects you to nod
- Ending a performance pattern that's rooted in fear

Then say this out loud: "I am not here to be controlled. I am here to serve with power and presence. I rise above, not because I'm better — but because I'm done abandoning myself."

Reflection

- Where have I confused survival with loyalty?
- Who am I when I'm not performing for approval?
- What boundaries will protect my leadership — even if no one else understands them?
- What is one truth I've been afraid to say out loud… even to myself?

You are allowed to choose you. Not in rebellion — but in reverence. Your healing is not a threat. It's a pattern-breaker. And when you stop performing for broken systems, you begin leading with a new kind of power — the kind that's rooted in wholeness, not hustle.

Part 3: Becoming a Healing Leader

"The home is the training ground of the soul. Lead there first, and the world will follow."

— Gloria A. Ramos

Chapter 8: Your Greatest Leadership Begins at Home

***"How you do anything is how you do everything."* — Martha Beck**

The Hidden Arena of Greatness

Leadership isn't defined by a title or a corner office. True leadership is influence. It's the daily practice of empowering others to grow, contribute, and align with a shared vision. And while many strive to lead in boardrooms, communities, or movements, our most lasting and impactful leadership often begins within the four walls of our own homes.

I've stood in boardrooms and behind podiums. I've negotiated policy, resolved conflicts, and helped shape systems. But none of it tested me like the sacred work of leading at home. When you strip away the audience, applause, or accolades, what's left is you—your patience, your truth, your ability to love when it's hard.

At home, leadership isn't about control—it's about connection. It means cultivating trust, setting clear values, and fostering a sense of collaboration where everyone's voice matters. Whether you're guiding a partner, raising children, caring for aging parents, or healing broken dynamics, the essence of leadership at home lies in your presence, your intention, and your example.

For those who hold leadership positions but feel unprepared or under-skilled, know this: leadership begins not with perfection, but with commitment. Adopting the role-model mindset—showing up as your best self, even when it's hard—is where transformation starts. It means having the courage to be consistent, the humility to grow, and the heart to serve with love.

The First Boardroom: Building Your Inner Circle with Vision

Leadership at home requires a kind of intimacy that public leadership often sidesteps. It isn't just about results, it's about how we achieve them. Harvard's Center on the Developing Child affirms that consistent, emotionally responsive relationships are foundational for developing resilience and life skills. This mirrors what John Maxwell calls the "Law of the Picture": people do what people see. Your home becomes your most honest mirror, and your first boardroom.

Transferable Power: The Traits That Travel Between Work and Home

The best leaders are integrated leaders. Traits like integrity, emotional regulation, vision, and adaptability aren't context-dependent—they are character-based. Carol Dweck's research on growth mindset reminds us that modeling behavior is one of the strongest ways to lead change. At home, modeling patience, curiosity, and humility in the face of stress teaches your family that leadership is not about perfection, but perseverance.

Resilient Families, Resilient Leaders

Families are ecosystems. When tension arises—financial strain, grief, trauma—leadership demands not just strength, but presence. Leadership during crisis isn't about suppressing emotion; it's about channeling clarity. Adaptive leaders set boundaries, communicate transparently, and create rituals of care. Something as simple as a Sunday dinner or a shared gratitude journal can stabilize a home and renew trust.

Women in the Arena: Leading with Grace in a World That Misreads It

Recent data from McKinsey's Women in the Workplace report shows that while women make up a growing share of leadership roles, they are still underrepresented at senior levels and face higher rates of burnout. Women are often expected to lead with assertiveness while maintaining likability—a nearly impossible paradox that penalizes both confidence and humility.

The challenges are more nuanced for women of color, who must often navigate both racial and gender bias simultaneously. This double burden can result in hypervigilance and overperformance, where rest feels like a liability and authenticity feels unsafe.

And yet, it is precisely these lived experiences that make women exceptional leaders. Women who lead from healed places—not hardened ones—carry the potential to reimagine leadership culture entirely. They challenge the old power paradigms that rely on dominance, and instead root their leadership in inclusion, intuition, and interdependence.

Women must be empowered not only to sit at the table but to reshape it—to redefine what strength, decisiveness, and grace look like when they co-exist. Leadership is not less effective when it is emotionally intelligent. In fact, according to Daniel Goleman's research, emotional intelligence accounts for nearly 90% of the difference between high performers and their peers.

The task now is not to ask women to change—but to change the environments that punish their authenticity. That shift begins at home, in how we parent daughters, how we model equality, and how we distribute emotional labor. When a woman leads a family with grace, she teaches future generations to lead without apology.

Her research supports the idea that vulnerability and empathy are not weaknesses in leadership—but vital sources of trust, authenticity, and transformative power.

Still, women face the unique challenge of being expected to lead like men in systems not built for them. This double-bind often forces women to harden. But strength does not always roar. Sometimes, it whispers in bedtime stories, negotiated peace over breakfast, or the ability to pause before reacting. Grace, especially in a world that demands performative toughness, is revolutionary.

Healing Begins at Home: From Inner Alignment to External Legacy

To lead a home well, one must first lead oneself. Inner alignment is the foundation of enduring influence. Without it, our leadership becomes reactive—shaped by the wounds we haven't healed, the habits we haven't questioned, and the roles we perform rather than inhabit.

Attachment theory helps illuminate this truth. The way we bond in childhood influences how we lead and relate in adulthood. Leaders who grew up with insecure attachment patterns may struggle with over-functioning, people-pleasing, or emotional withdrawal. But healing is possible—and necessary.

Healing leadership doesn't mean hiding your struggles; it means integrating them. It means becoming curious about your triggers, conscious of your coping strategies, and committed to rewriting your internal narrative. It means asking not, "What's wrong with me?" but "What happened to me—and what do I need now to lead with wholeness?"

This kind of work requires support. Whether through coaching, therapy, spiritual mentorship, or honest self-reflection, the leader who invests in their own healing multiplies their impact. Why? Because they stop leaking stress and start channeling safety.

High performance is not fueled by overdrive, but by alignment—by living in step with your values, maintaining emotional clarity, and creating relational peace. When your personal integrity is intact, your leadership becomes sustainable and deeply influential.

The Hardest Leadership of My Life

During the most harrowing three years of my life, leadership was not optional; it was survival.

My mother was hospitalized in a subacute care facility, intubated and unable to speak, fighting COPD while my family fought on her behalf daily. For three years, she didn't have a voice—so I became her voice. I fought fiercely as the primary caregiver—managing her care while also supporting my 92-year-old grandmother, my ailing father, raising a six-year-old daughter, and navigating my own high-risk pregnancy.

At the same time, I was laid off from my job. I was a single mother. I was serving as an elected school board member during one of the most politically contentious periods in our district's history. And shortly after giving birth, I was diagnosed with cancerous lesions that required urgent medical attention, adding yet another layer of physical and emotional trauma.

I wasn't just stretched thin. I was being reshaped.

In those years, anger was my go-to fuel. It gave me the edge I needed to advocate fiercely, to push through injustice, to wake up and keep going. But eventually, that fire began to burn through the very reserves I needed to sustain myself. What had once protected me became corrosive.

Surrender came slowly—because for years, survival demanded I stay in control. But control is not the same as power. And eventually, I had to face that my white-knuckled endurance was no longer serving me. I began releasing the idea that I had to do it all, fix it all, hold it all. And in its place, I reached for faith—not the performative kind, but the kind that lets you fall apart and still be held.

I began to make peace with what I couldn't fix. I stopped fighting every battle with urgency and started choosing presence over panic. My prayers became less about changing outcomes and more about finding the strength to stay soft when I wanted to armor up.

This wasn't spiritual bypassing; it was spiritual grounding. It allowed me to carry grief, joy, exhaustion, and courage at the same time. That's what home leadership taught me: that the hardest things don't always get easier, but we get stronger in how we carry them.

Gradually, I began to replace my anger with stillness. I chose reflection over reaction. I gave myself permission to soften—not as surrender, but as sacred self-respect. In that tenderness, I found the strength I had never known before.

No amount of title or influence could carry the weight of those years. I had to become a steward of everyone's well-being while still learning how to ask for help of my own. I had to lead without reward, advocate without certainty, and show up with grace even when I had no reserves left.

And yet, through those years, a deeper leadership was being formed in me. The kind that doesn't come with applause or recognition, but with integrity forged in quiet decisions. The kind of leadership that teaches you how to prioritize dignity over urgency. Presence over panic. Faith over fear.

It was in those moments of exhaustion and decision fatigue that I came to understand this: home leadership is not just a personal matter—it is a spiritual practice. It is legacy in motion.

I didn't just survive that chapter. I emerged with clarity on what matters: protecting my peace, honoring my truth, and never again abandoning myself to meet someone else's expectations. I lead differently now—because I've led through the fire.

Leaving a Positive Lasting Imprint

Before we can leave a mark in the world, we must ask what mark we're leaving in our homes. Our children may never remember the awards we won—but they'll never forget how we made them feel. The energy we bring home is our leadership fingerprint. What kind of imprint are we leaving?

The Greatest Leadership Begins at Home

Activation

Activation Exercise:

Create a 7-day "Home Leadership Audit." Each day, write down one moment you showed up with strength, grace, or heart—like choosing patience over criticism, or pausing to really listen instead of rushing ahead. Identify one area you want to strengthen. By the end of the week, reflect on how your energy influenced your home environment. Then ask: what do I want my leadership legacy to be here?

Reflection

- Where do I lead from control rather than connection?
- How can I bring more presence and intention to my home life?

Chapter 9: Holographic Thinking: Leadership Reflected in Every Part of You

"A person must live as if something deeper were at stake than merely surviving.

***The true self longs to become visible, to be seen and known."* —Michael Meade**

The Frame of a New Reality

Leadership isn't something you turn on when the cameras are rolling or the minutes are being taken. Real leadership shows up everywhere—how you speak to yourself in the dark, how you de-escalate tension without collapsing your truth, how you live your values when no one else is watching. This is holographic thinking: the understanding that who you are in one space reflects across every other. Nothing is isolated. Everything is connected.

We were taught to compartmentalize. At home, we're caretakers. At work, we're professionals. In our communities, we become the responsible ones. But fragmentation isn't leadership, it's survival. And many of us, especially those healing from childhood betrayal trauma, have built success by fragmenting ourselves. We become high-performing in public, but unfulfilled in private. We pour into others because we haven't yet learned to receive from ourselves.

But a fragmented leader can't build a whole legacy. Integration is the turning point. When you begin to see your choices, your energy, your values, and your identity as a coherent whole, you stop performing and start transforming. You lead not from a mask, but from meaning. You don't chase outcomes—you embody presence. That's when healing becomes legacy. That's when legacy becomes a living mirror.

In this final chapter, we return to the whole. To the place where service, leadership, and healing become indistinguishable. You'll learn how to embody your values in every domain—not just to feel congruent, but to create impact that multiplies. Because when your leadership flows from alignment instead of adaptation, you don't just influence others.

You heal generations.

Holographic Vantage Point —Seeing the Whole Without Losing the Parts

When you zoom out from the noise and into the truth, a different picture begins to form. You're not just a person with problems. You're a living expression of every story you've survived. Your brilliance, your grief, your mistakes, they're all part of something larger. A lineage. A legacy. A movement.

This is holographic thinking: the realization that your leadership, your healing, your daily choices all matter—and not in isolation, but in interaction.

You are not healing in a vacuum. You are reshaping history.

But far too many leaders keep leading from the same wound they're trying to transcend. They speak from scar tissue. They confuse anger for discernment. They lead from a posture of edge instead of presence. And in doing so, they replay old stories with new titles.

On the other extreme, some leaders mistake kindness for avoidance. They stay agreeable with the very people who harmed them. They call it forgiveness, but really, it's fear dressed up as grace. They call it being "the bigger person," but it's often the result of believing they don't deserve boundaries.

Holographic leadership invites you to stop swinging between extremes. You don't have to dominate to be strong or disappear to be kind. You don't have to prove your wholeness—you can live it.

Wholeness doesn't need applause. It generates energy. It creates culture. It turns your presence into healing.

Leading Beyond the Mask

We all wear masks. Some helped us survive, especially in environments that weren't safe for our full selves. The high-achiever mask. The peacemaker masks. The expert mask. At some point, they protected us.

But the mask that protected you yesterday might be limiting you today.

Part of evolving as a leader is recognizing when you've outgrown your mask. What once kept you safe now keeps you small. What once got you into rooms now blocks your authenticity.

Leading beyond the mask means choosing vulnerability. Not oversharing. Not collapsing. But being real. Present. Honest. It means you stop curating connections and start creating it. You stop leading from performance and start leading from truth.

And people feel it.

Your team, your partner, your children—they feel the shift. They trust what's real. They lean into what's embodied. Your leadership becomes breathable again. Spacious. Energizing.

In *Chapter 2*, we talked about self-awareness being the root of leadership. That lesson arrives here again. Because to remove the mask, you have to know who you are underneath it. Not the version that performs for validation—but the version whom leads with conviction.

That's the real leader. That's the one we've been waiting for.

The Solitude of Integrity

Leadership isn't always celebrated. Sometimes, it's a quiet, gut-wrenching decision. Sometimes, it's doing the right thing with no witnesses, no rewards, and no backup.

I'll never forget the night I voted against something everyone else supported. I knew it wasn't aligned. I knew it would hurt my credibility. And I did it anyway. Not because I wanted to be difficult. But because integrity is not a brand—it's a backbone.

I left that meeting in silence. No one looked me in the eye. No one clapped. But I slept that night with peace in my chest. And my children watched me do the right thing even when it cost me influence.

That is legacy.

The solitude of integrity is a crucible. It reveals who you are when the crowd disappears. And if you're doing leadership right, you will experience it.

It's the moment when *Chapter 6* comes to life—when ego and impact go head-to-head, and you choose principle over performance.

But here's the thing: solitude doesn't mean abandonment. It means refinement. It strips you down to your essence. And from that place, your leadership becomes clean. Powerful. Untouchable.

You stop needing the room to affirm you. You become the room.

Building a Healing Legacy Through Holographic Leadership

Leadership isn't what you do. It's who you are becoming.

A healing legacy is built in moments people don't see. It's in how you apologize. How you show your kids how to regulate. How you remember your ancestors. How you honor the women who came before you. It's how you spend your money. How you protect your health. How you prioritize love.

Your legacy is the pattern you live every day. Not the speech you give once. Not the résumé you polish. Not the project you launch for optics.

In *Chapter 5*, we explored what it means to build for generations. Holographic leadership carries that forward. It recognizes that your actions are not isolated; they're spiritual and systemic.

Your healed leadership becomes a template. For your children. Your community. Your lineage. Even for people who will never know your name—but will inherit your energy.

In *Chapter 8*, we talked about leading at home. This is the natural continuation. Because the way you tend to your household, your health, and your spirit, becomes the vibration you carry into every room.

You don't have to be perfect. You must be integrated.

Holographic leadership doesn't mean you always get it right. It means you lead from the whole story, not just the highlight reel.

It means you're not just healing for yourself. You're healing the system. You're healing the story. You're healing the legacy.

Becoming the Best Version of Yourself

Activation: Integrate to Impact

Choose one place this week to lead differently. Maybe it's your boardroom. Your kitchen. Your relationship. Take one integrated action: a truth you tell, a habit you release, a boundary you enforce, a moment you reclaim.

Let it be real. Let it be full. Let it be holy.

Write it down. This is your holographic leadership in motion. This is how you become the ancestor your future family will thank.

Reflection

Where are you still divided within yourself? What are the roles, habits, or reactions that no longer reflect your truth?

Ask yourself:

- Where do I still lead from fear instead of alignment?
- What mask am I ready to lay down—for good?
- What part of me needs to be reintegrated to lead from love, not performance?

Closing Benediction

May your life no longer be led by the echoes of
survival, but by the sacred rhythm of who you've
become. May every scar remind you of your strength,
and every boundary you now keep, your rebirth.
Let your presence be your protest.
Let your softness be your strategy.
Let your joy be the proof that healing took root.

You are not here to perform wholeness.
You are here to *live it*—loudly, quietly, imperfectly,
and fully.
May your legacy be stitched from truth, not titles.
And may the future you're building
rise from everything you've reclaimed.

About the Author

Gloria A. Ramos is a Certified High Performance Coach™, bestselling author, and elected official with over two decades of leadership in education, community advocacy, and transformational coaching. As a mother, public servant, and legacy-builder, Gloria specializes in helping high-achieving individuals—especially those healing from childhood betrayal trauma—reclaim their clarity, courage, and capacity for meaningful change.

After surviving a life-threatening health crisis and years of burnout from over-functioning in leadership roles, Gloria rebuilt her life from the inside out. She has since helped hundreds of leaders break generational patterns, lead from authenticity, and create impact that begins at home and echoes through institutions.

Blending soul-deep healing with real-world strategy, Gloria equips her clients to turn pain into purpose and performance into legacy. Her work empowers readers and clients alike to lead lives that are not just successful—but soul-aligned, sustainable, and sacred.

Acknowledgments

To write a book like this—part memoir, part handbook, part healing manifesto—is to stand on the shoulders of many.

To my husband, thank you for your unwavering belief in me. You saw the fire in me even when I only saw smoke. Your love, strength, and constant support have given me room to breathe, rise, and lead fully.

To my children, you are my greatest why. Every page of this book carries the weight of my promise to love you, protect you, and lead you with honesty and hope. You teach me every day what it means to lead with purpose.

To the leaders who mentored me, challenged me, or betrayed me—thank you. Every experience sharpened my voice, tested my resolve, and pushed me to choose clarity over chaos, integrity over comfort.

To my community—the readers, clients, students, and souls who trust me with their transformation—thank you for showing up. For daring to heal. For doing the work that others are afraid to do. This book is for you.

To my ancestors and foremothers—thank you for enduring more than I'll ever know. I carry your legacy and write your strength into every chapter.

And to God—my source, my center, my strategist—I could never have written a single word without You.

Legacy in Motion: The Healing Leadership Toolkit

This toolkit is more than a collection of exercises. It's your bridge from leadership theory to embodied transformation. Each tool corresponds with a chapter in Lead with Purpose, offering a deeper, more intentional practice than the chapter's reflection prompts alone. These tools are designed to:

- Move you from insight into integration
- Align with one of the Six High Performance Habits
- Activate your healing leadership from the inside out

Use these practices to realign, refuel, recalibrate, and rebuild. Some you'll return to often. Others will serve as turning points. Either way, they will help you lead with integrity and legacy—in your body, relationships, decisions, and systems.

TOOL #1: Raise Your Standard

Linked High Performance Habit: Raise Necessity
Relevant Chapter: Chapter 1 — Leadership Is About Service

What This Unlocks

This tool helps you reconnect with what's truly at stake in your leadership. It transforms passive intention into personal necessity—so your vision becomes non-negotiable.

When to Use It
- When you're doubting your impact
- When your motivation feels low
- When your goals feel disconnected from your real life

How to Use It
1. On a blank page, write: "I must become the kind of leader who..." and complete the sentence. Do this five times.

2. Then ask: "Who is counting on me to live out this version of myself?" Name specific people or communities.

3. Write: "What happens if I don't?" Be honest.
4. Post your completed statements somewhere visible for one week. Read them every morning.

Reflection

Have I made my mission optional—or urgent?

TOOL #2: Architect Your Beliefs

Linked High Performance Habit: Seek Clarity
Relevant Chapter: Chapter 2 — Beliefs and Self-Awareness

What This Unlocks

This tool helps you examine and rewire the belief architecture that silently governs your leadership. Until you name the hidden agreements shaping your identity, you will lead from limitation, not liberation.

When to Use It
- When you feel stuck in unhelpful leadership cycles
- When self-doubt or people-pleasing resurfaces
- When a success doesn't feel satisfying
- When you feel disconnected from your purpose

How to Use It
1. Identify a repeating leadership pattern.
2. Ask: "What would someone have to believe for this to feel normal?"
3. Ask: "Whose voice is this really?" Declare: "This belief does not belong to me."
4. Write new identity-level beliefs: "I am the kind of leader who..."
5. Speak one new belief aloud each morning for a week.

Reflection Prompt

What belief have I been living that no longer reflects who I am—or who I'm becoming?

TOOL #3: Spark Forward

Linked High Performance Habit: Generate Energy
Relevant Chapter: Chapter 3 — Catalytic Leadership

What This Unlocks

Catalytic leaders don't lead by force. They lead by fire—the kind that ignites belief in others. This tool helps you access and apply your natural spark.

When to Use It
- When you forget your own influence
- When you're tempted to control rather than empower
- When someone near you is stuck or doubting
- When you want to restore energy and inspiration in a group dynamic

How to Use It
1. Write about someone you helped rise.
2. Identify your 3 catalytic strengths.
3. Choose a "spark word" and declare it each morning.
4. Take one action this week to activate someone else.

Reflection Prompt

Am I hoarding my light—or multiplying it?

TOOL #4: Ignite the Shift

Linked High Performance Habit: Generate Energy
Relevant Chapter: Chapter 4 — Adaptive Leadership

What This Unlocks

This tool helps you move from emotional burnout into purposeful energy. When you're stuck, stalled, or shrinking yourself, this practice reignites your internal momentum and activates catalytic leadership from within.

When to Use It

- When you feel emotionally flat, overextended, or dulled
- When you're leading something new but feel unsure of yourself
- When you want to shift from passivity into power

How to Use It

1. Write down a moment in your life when you made something move — a time you lit the fire. What sparked it? What shifted in you?
2. Now write: "What part of me have I dimmed that is ready to re-ignite?"
3. Choose a catalytic word for your week. (Examples: Fire. Motion. Disrupt. Charge. Rise.) Say it aloud every morning with one deep breath.

4. Pick one action that scares you and excites you — and take the first step today. Small is fine. Just move.

Reflection Prompt

What's the cost of staying dimmed when you were born to catalyze?

TOOL #5: The Power Anchor

Linked High Performance Habit: Increase Productivity
Relevant Chapter: Chapter 5 — Generational Leadership

What This Unlocks

This tool helps you focus your energy on what matters most — especially in moments of stress, distraction, or shifting priorities. It aligns your action with intention so you lead from presence, not panic.

When to Use It

- When your schedule feels overloaded
- When external demands threaten your priorities
- When you want to lead with discipline and grace

How to Use It

1. At the start of your week, write down:
    - One thing I must complete
    - One thing I will protect (boundary, energy, time)
    - One thing I will release (distraction, obligation, or perfectionism)
1. Choose a 30-minute block today to move the must forward. No multitasking. No postponing.
2. At the end of the day, reflect: “Did I lead from alignment — or urgency?”

3. Repeat weekly to track patterns, clarify distractions, and protect your core commitments.

Reflection Prompt

Where am I pouring energy that doesn't return clarity, impact, or peace?

TOOL #6: Courage Capsule

Linked High Performance Habit: Demonstrate Courage

Relevant Chapter: Chapter 6 — When Leadership Wounds Instead of Heals

What This Unlocks

This tool helps you practice courageous leadership through micro-actions that expand your tolerance for discomfort and truth-telling. These 'courage capsules' are daily or weekly practices you can adopt to build brave momentum.

When to Use It

- When you've been avoiding a conversation, decision, or truth
- When fear is guiding your leadership more than values
- When you want to expand your integrity and visibility

How to Use It
Choose one or more to practice this week:

- Speak up in a meeting where you'd normally stay silent.
- Have a hard conversation you've been avoiding.
- Share your story vulnerably with someone you trust.

- Set a firm boundary—even if it disappoints someone.
- Make a decision that aligns with your values, not just your fears.

Reflection Prompt

What am I afraid of that's worth moving toward anyway?

TOOL #7: Healing Inventory

Linked High Performance Habit: Develop Influence
Relevant Chapter: Chapter 7 — Recognizing and Rising Above Toxic Leadership
What This Unlocks

This tool is designed to help you confront and clear hidden emotional debris that distorts your leadership energy. When you lead from unhealed pain, you unconsciously recreate emotional patterns that block trust and dim your influence. This tool helps you name it, feel it, and begin to release it.

When to Use It

- When your leadership feels reactive or guarded
- When you sense unresolved hurt affecting your communication
- When you want to lead with more emotional freedom and generosity

How to Use It

1. Who (or what) still has power over your emotions today because of something unresolved?
2. What recurring story do you tell yourself about this pain?
3. What part of you is still holding on for protection—and what part of you is ready to release it?

4. What would healing look like, feel like, or sound like in this area of your life?

Now, declare this aloud or write it down in your own words: “I am not my wound. I am my willingness to heal.”

Reflection Prompt

What am I still carrying that no longer belongs to the leader I am becoming?

TOOL #8: Family Alignment Map

Linked High Performance Habit: Demonstrate Courage Relevant Chapter: Chapter 8 — Your Greatest Leadership Begins at Home

What This Unlocks

This tool helps you realign your leadership at home by clarifying values, improving communication, and honoring boundaries. It's not about managing people—it's about cultivating trust, emotional safety, and mutual respect.

When to Use It

- When home life feels disconnected or strained
- When your leadership persona is different at home than in public
- When you're ready to lead your family with more intentionality

How to Use It

Set aside time for personal reflection or to engage with your family in dialogue around the following prompts:

1. What are the 3 core values you want your household to reflect?
2. How does your current behavior at home align with those values?
3. Where are you leading from love, and where are you leading from fear?
4. What does grace look like in your parenting, partnership, or caregiving?

5. Where do boundaries need to be clarified to protect the emotional health of the home?

Take Action:
- Choose one small action this week that brings your home into better alignment with your core values.
- Communicate your intention clearly and lovingly to at least one person in your home.

Reflection Prompt

Does my home feel like a refuge, a reflection— or a performance?

TOOL #9: The Holographic Audit

Linked High Performance Habit: Seek Clarity
Relevant Chapter: Chapter 9 — Holographic Thinking

What This Unlocks

This tool invites you to assess your life holistically—through the lens of legacy, integration, and alignment. It reveals where you're compartmentalizing and helps you lead as a whole, not in fragments.

When to Use It
- When something feels “off” but you can’t name what
- When your actions feel misaligned with your deeper values
- When you’re ready to lead from coherence, not compartmentalization

How to Use It
Using the five domains below, rate each area of your life from 1 (out of alignment) to 10 (fully aligned).
Then reflect:
1. Personal Health: Is your body cared for in a way that supports your longevity and vitality?
2. Relationships: Are your connections mutual, nourishing, and emotionally honest?
3. Work and Mission: Is your work an expression of your soul—or a performance that drains you?
4. Finances: Are your financial choices creating freedom or hiding misalignment?
5. Spirituality: Do you feel grounded in presence, meaning, and truth?

After scoring:
- Identify the one domain most out of alignment.
- Write: What would a 10 look like here—and what's one step I can take toward it this week?

Reflection Prompt

Am I building a life I can stand inside of—or one I have to escape from?

BONUS TOOL: Action Indicator Assessment

What This Unlocks

This assessment gives you a snapshot of your readiness and ability to commit to a meaningful goal. It reveals gaps in motivation, capacity, or support before they derail your follow-through.

When to Use It

- When you're deciding whether to pursue a new goal or pivot
- When you're setting quarterly intentions or strategic outcomes
- When you're feeling blocked and unsure why

How to Use It

Rate each of the ten categories below from 1 to 10:

1. Future Identity – Is this goal aligned with who you are becoming?
2. Intrinsic Value – Does this goal feel meaningful beyond external rewards?
3. Utilitarian Value – Will this goal create real, useful outcomes?
4. Opportunity Cost – Can you pursue it without sacrificing what matters most?
5. Delay Time – Will you see results soon enough to stay motivated?
6. Personal Control – Can you directly influence the outcome with your actions?
7. Social Support – Do you have the encouragement or partnership you need?

8. Bandwidth Belief – Do you believe you have the time and energy to do this well?
9. Resource Availability – Do you have (or can access) what's needed to succeed?
10. Autonomy – Will you be free to lead and make decisions as needed?

Total Score: ______

Interpretation
If your score is below 75, don't abandon the goal—strengthen your strategy. Focus on any category scoring below 8 and ask:
- What would help me raise this score?
- Is this goal in alignment with what I truly want—or am I chasing someone else's version of success?

Use this tool to clarify and sharpen your focus.

Toolkit Complete. Continue to revisit and revise as you grow. These tools aren't just exercises; they're mirrors, measuring sticks, and launchpads for your healing legacy.

Gloria A. Ramos helps high-achieving leaders transform private pain into purposeful power. Through The Heartful Hero, her 12-week signature program, she guides clients to reclaim clarity, embodiment, and legacy—in leadership, relationships, and life.

Ready to take the next step?

Book your Discovery Call at:

Gloria@GloriaRamos.com

GloriaRamos.com
310-713-7485